THE GAME CHANGER

8 Tips for Men to Find Peace

Coach John Louden

LEVAS Publishing

ISBN-13 (eBook): 979-8-9898692-0-6
ISBN-13 (Print): 979-8-9898692-1-3

Published by: LEVAS Publishing
Cover design by: LEVAS Publishing
Printed in the United States of America

This book is dedicated to my family and friends who have supported me through all my trials and tribulations, especially my wife and children who love me unconditionally. In loving memory of Erdell Bunche, Carl A. Bunche Sr., Gerald Bunche Jr., Beverly Bunche, Alia Reeves, Maggie Reeves, Jeff Tyson, and Linda Asim, whose love and support I will forever cherish. I am also grateful to the countless relatives, friends, and mentors who have guided, stood by, and spiritually-supported me when I needed it most. I am tremendously thankful for the unconditional love and understanding from all those close to me.

This is for everyone who has ever struggled - you can win.

Sincerely, Coach John Louden

CONTENTS

PREFACE

In a world filled with challenges and expectations, men often find themselves grappling with the pressures of life in silence. In "The Game Changer," author and coach, John Louden (known as the Concrete Genius) provides a heartfelt and insightful guide for men seeking to navigate their journey towards inner peace and fulfillment.

Drawing from his personal experiences and a wealth of wisdom, Coach Louden presents eight essential tips that address various aspects of a man's life. From prioritizing self-care and building meaningful relationships to focusing on purpose and embracing positive lifestyle changes, each chapter offers actionable advice that encourages personal growth and transformation.

Louden's candid and down-to-earth approach resonates with readers as he delves into the challenges men often face, including health concerns, self- doubt, and societal pressures. Through relatable anecdotes and practical suggestions, he empowers men to overcome obstacles, forge strong connections, and make choices that lead to a more balanced and harmonious life.

"The Game Changer" is not just a book; it's a compassionate companion that acknowledges the struggles men encounter and offers a path towards resilience, confidence, and tranquility. Whether you're a young adult setting out on your journey or a seasoned individual seeking a renewed sense of purpose, this book is a heartfelt invitation to find peace and purpose in every facet of life.

Discover how to navigate challenges, harness your potential, and embrace a life of contentment. Let "The Game Changer" guide you on a transformative journey towards inner peace and fulfillment.

INTRODUCTION

Hello, I'm Coach John Louden, your author and coach, also known as the Concrete Genius. It's an absolute honor to have you here, reading this book today. Let's start by acknowledging that God has been good to us. If you're here, reading or listening to these words, you're truly blessed. Remember, every day you're alive is a blessing in itself.

As we dive into this, let's take a moment to appreciate the day - it's a beautiful Monday, the weekend was amazing. I managed to check off quite a few things from my to-do list, spent quality time with my family, especially since it was my son's last weekend before he embarked on his college journey.

These times are both heartwarming and bittersweet. You want nothing but the best for your child, but you can't help but feel a pang of longing as they step out into the world. Yet, this is how growth happens. Kids leave the nest, learn from their experiences (or from others' experiences), and set out on their path to greatness. Just like my son and my entire family, anyone who's part of my movement is dedicated to chasing greatness.

Without further ado, let's talk about something significant: growth. Growth is always essential, whether it's about basketball, parenting, or personal development. In this book, though, I wanted to focus on something specifically for men. This past year has been enlightening for me. Many of my male friends have faced challenges--illness, depression, health concerns, and the general struggles that men often endure silently.

But here's the thing--it doesn't have to be that way. With this book, I'm going to share eight tips broken down into eight chapters that I believe can help men find peace and navigate through life's challenges with strength. So, gentlemen, this one's for you. Let's get started on this journey of self- improvement and empowerment.

CHAPTER 1

Find What You Love & Make It A Career

The secret sauce to a man's tranquility, often missed in the hustle of life, is straightforward—self-care. It's the bedrock of our well-being, yet it's astonishing how we let it slip through the cracks.

Caught in the whirlwind of work, family obligations, and life's incessant demands, our needs are pushed aside, sometimes without a second thought.

But let's get real for a minute. Running on fumes, you can't be there for anyone else effectively. I've walked this tightrope and learned the hard way. In the early days of my coaching career, I was all in, dedicating every ounce of energy to the kids I mentored. My schedule was a relentless stream of practices, games, and team events, with scarcely a moment to myself.

The initial rush of making a difference was electric. However, as time ticked on, that zest started to wane. Exhaustion took over, irritability crept in, and my family felt like they were on the backburner. My own self-care was non-existent—I was skimping on meals, sleep, and personal time, and it took a toll on my health and relationships.

That was my wake-up call. I had to pivot my approach to self-care. It began with a simple 15-minute morning ritual to ground myself and map out my day. I weaved in mindfulness and deep breathing exercises whenever stress tried to get the upper hand.

Learning to say 'no' became my mantra when things got too hectic. I found that being a present and supportive mentor didn't mean attending every single event. Delegating to my assistant coaches also became part of my strategy to dodge burnout.

The game-changer, though? Embracing the joy in life. It dawned on me how vital it is to cherish family time and leisure. Hobbies and downtime weren't just fillers—they were essential. Date nights, unplugged family evenings, and pursuing personal interests like fishing or restoring vintage cars became non-negotiables.

Self-care also meant indulging in massages, taking mental health days when the tank was low, and reconnecting with nature through hikes. It wasn't overnight, but I learned to give myself the green light to decelerate. Now, self-care isn't an add-on; it's part of the fabric of my life.

So, take a hard look at your daily grind. Are you overloading yourself without breathing room? Do you often skip the essentials like proper meals, exercise, and sleep?

If hobbies and relaxation are foreign concepts to you, it's time for a change. Self-care isn't indulgent—it's essential.

Kick-off with simple, daily routines—a morning meditation, nutritious meals, and a fixed bedtime. Draw boundaries firmly and nix the non- essentials. Remember, there's strength in reaching out. Sharing your needs with your partner or close friends can alleviate stress.

Prioritizing self-care renews your energy and patience for all facets of life. It's about finding balance, building resilience, and nurturing inner peace. Carve out time for yourself—it's worth its weight in gold.

Now, let's get tactical with self-care strategies. Start with a personal audit. Are you clocking in 7-8 hours of sleep, staying active, eating healthily, and taking regular breaks from the grind? Neglecting these basics can wear down even the sturdiest of us. Address these first.

Stress check next. If 'overwhelmed' is your middle name, it's time to explore stress management practices like breathwork, yoga, and therapy. Don't shoulder it all—lean on your community. And don't forget to indulge in your passions and hobbies—they're not just fun; they refuel your soul.

Here's a list of self-care hacks to give you a leg up:

- Sneak in micro-pauses during your day to reset your brain.
- Even a minute counts.
- Block self-care time on your calendar—it's as important as any meeting.
- Shake up your workout routine—variety keeps it fresh and exciting.
- Plan date nights and outings with your partner to reconnect and unwind.
- Consider massages or acupuncture for physical rejuvenation.
- Dial down on social media and electronic devices periodically.
- Surround yourself with nature; it has a way of soothing the soul.
- Seek professional help like counseling if you're grappling with specific issues.

Self-care needs to be more than a one-off—it's a lifestyle. Adapt and refine your methods, but keep the consistency. Be proactive, not reactive, and tailor your self-care to your individual needs and circumstances. And remember, it's a journey—aim for progress, not perfection.

Starting might feel like an uphill battle, but with time, self-care will become second nature. Enjoy the discovery process of understanding yourself better. A robust self-care regimen is the cornerstone for everything else in life. Your well-being is the best investment you can make—the returns are immeasurable.

CHAPTER 2
Forgiving Yourself

We men often aim for the stars, setting standards so high they're near impossible to reach. We expect to be unflinching providers, handling life's every twist and turn with a steadfast resolve. But what happens when we stumble and our reach falls short? That's when self-criticism often kicks in, relentless and unforgiving, as we chastise ourselves for the missteps we've made.

I've been caught in that storm of self-critique, too. In my younger years, anger and impetuosity were at the helm, leading me to make decisions that hurt those I cared about. The severity of my temper was matched only by the intensity of my self-imposed pressure to be flawless. This concoction of rage and the pursuit of perfection left a trail of regret and guilt that I carried for far too long.

The turning point was the realization that I needed to embrace self- forgiveness. Fixating on my faults, endlessly replaying them, was like sabotaging myself—blocking any path to growth or happiness. Self- forgiveness is not merely a gift but a necessity for healing and moving forward. It allows us to break free from the shackles of past mistakes and grow into better men, partners, and leaders.

To forgive oneself is to stop the internal war of guilt and shame. These emotions can eat away at our spirit, paving the way for bitterness and resentment. You can't give others the love or support they need if you're bound by self-contempt.

For me, learning to forgive myself was transformative. It softened my edges, infused patience into my actions, and deepened my compassion. The journey begins with owning up to our mistakes, confronting them head-on without excuses. It's about peering into the reasons behind our actions, understanding the pain or anger that may have driven them, and acknowledging the impact they've had on others.

Apologies and reparations are important, though they don't erase the past —they pave a path toward healing. But what's crucial is to use these errors as stepping stones towards better decisions in the future. Remember, self- forgiveness isn't about excusing repetitive mistakes; it's about evolving from them.

This path requires patience and resilience. Our ingrained habits and defensive mindsets won't change overnight. There will be setbacks, but it's essential to keep striving for self-improvement. Self-forgiveness isn't just about letting go of the past; it's about releasing yourself to a future where you're not defined by your lowest moments but inspired by the lessons they've taught you.

The liberation that comes with self-forgiveness can propel you to new heights, opening doors to possibilities previously shut by your own hand. It's like finding yourself in front of a vast ocean of opportunity; the horizon is wide and the path uncharted. Self-forgiveness allows you to set sail, free from the heavy anchors of deepest regrets.

Imagine the person you could become when not weighed down by the chains of past mistakes. This freedom can elevate your life in ways you might not yet envision—mending relationships, pursuing passions once deemed unattainable, or simply living with an inner peace that radiates outward, affecting all you do. Let go of the burdens that hold you down and allow yourself the space to soar into this expansive sky of potential.

Yet, as invigorating as this liberation is, the climb to the summit of self- forgiveness can be steep and treacherous. The journey is not a straight ascent. There will be ledges where you'll need to rest, patches of rough terrain that will challenge your resolve, and moments when the peak seems shrouded in an impenetrable mist. It's in these times that old, destructive thoughts may emerge like hidden crevasses, threatening to plunge you back into the abyss of self-condemnation.

I know this mountain well. It's rugged, intimidating, and can seem insurmountable. But every step upward, every small victory, every moment you choose to not let the destructive thoughts win, fortifies your spirit. The climb is not just about reaching the top —it's about transforming with each step, growing stronger, more resilient, and more compassionate with yourself.

So how does one navigate such a challenging ascent? Here are some pragmatic steps to help you on this journey:

1. **Anchor Yourself in the Present:** Begin by grounding yourself in the now. Your power lies in the present moment, not in the shadows of yesterday or the uncertainties of tomorrow. Whenever you find your mind wandering back to past errors, gently but firmly guide it back to where you are and what you're doing.

2. **Map Your Progress**: Keep a journal of your journey towards self-forgiveness. Document not just the missteps, but also the moments of clarity and forgiveness. Over time, you'll see how far you've climbed.

3. **Equip Yourself with Knowledge**: Understand the psychological patterns that lead to self-criticism. Learn about the triggers and the origins of your harsh self-judgment. Knowledge is like the right gear for the climb; it makes the journey safer and more doable.

4. **Set up Camps of Self-Care**: Just as a climber needs base camps to rest and acclimate, establish regular practices of self-care. This could be meditation, exercise, or engaging in hobbies that bring you joy—anything that replenishes your spirit.

5. **Seek Guides and Companions**: You don't have to climb alone. Seek out friends, family, therapists, or support groups. These individuals can be like sherpas and fellow climbers, providing support and perspective as you ascend.

6. **Celebrate Your Elevation**: Acknowledge and celebrate the distance you've covered. Each act of self-forgiveness, no matter how small, is a step upward. These moments of celebration are like clearings on a mountain that offer stunning views of the valleys below.

7. **Be Prepared for the Descent**: There may be times you need to descend to old memories and feelings—not to stay, but to understand and heal. With the right tools and support, you can revisit these depths safely, taking what you learn back up to higher ground.

8. **Trust in Your Ability to Climb**: Have faith in your capacity to reach the summit of self-forgiveness. Trust that with each step, you are becoming the person you are meant to be.

The climb towards self-forgiveness may be one of the most arduous treks you'll undertake, but it is also one of the most rewarding. With each step, you will shed the weights that hinder you, and with each milestone, you will gain a lighter heart. In this journey, there is no insurmountable peak, only the constant pursuit of growth, understanding, and the boundless compassion you are capable of extending to yourself.

I know self-forgiveness can be a tough mountain to climb, especially when those old, destructive thoughts try to claw their way back in. Here are some pragmatic steps to help you on this journey:

- Write down your regrets and then physically discard them as a symbolic act of letting go.
- Speak affirmations of forgiveness to yourself - positive reinforcement is powerful.
- Transform negative self-talk into a nurturing inner voice.
- Look to your spiritual beliefs or practices for strength in releasing past burdens.
- If your struggles run deep, don't hesitate to seek counseling or join a support group.
- Channel your energy toward constructive actions, not dwelling on the wrongs.
- Practice mindfulness—when guilt tries to re-enter, gently guide your thoughts back to the present.
- Reaffirm your commitment to living according to your values each day, so you're not defined by past missteps.
- Recognize that while past pains influenced your choices, they don't have to dictate your future.

Self-forgiveness is a testament to your courage and your will to persevere. Yes, you will falter at times, but with dedication, you'll also rise. The path to peace and the man you aspire to become await on the other side of forgiveness. Grant yourself that peace. The rest is still unwritten, and with self-forgiveness, your story can take a turn toward the remarkable.

Remember: You are worthy of peace. Your past errors don't have to cast a shadow over your future. We all carry regrets, but we also hold the power to step beyond them. Forgive yourself and embrace the boundless opportunities that come with it.

CHAPTER 3

Focus On Your Purpose

Alright, let's get into it – finding what gets you ticking, what stirs you to hop out of bed before the alarm even buzzes. That thing is what some folks call your 'purpose.' It's more than just what you do; it's what you're meant to do. It gives a reason to your daily grind, makes it more than just a grind.

Took me a while, but I realized my thing was helping kids find their way, especially on the basketball court. I didn't just wake up one day and figure it out, though. It was a gradual thing, a feeling that grew stronger every time I coached my son and his friends. I was doing more than just calling plays; I was part of their lives, and that felt right.

When I clocked this was my purpose, I didn't just mess around with it when I had spare time. I dived headfirst. I hit the books, connected with other coaches, personalized training plans for each of the kids. It was my main gig, even if it wasn't paying the bills.

This meant giving up lazy weekends, skipping out on after-work drinks to study game footage instead. Because this wasn't just a hobby anymore, it was my purpose. And that meant all-in, no half-measures.

Finding and sticking to your purpose will separate you from the folks who are just talking a big game. Once you pinpoint what lights a fire in you, go after it with everything you've got. It's not gonna be a cakewalk, for sure. You'll have to tune out the background noise, keep pushing through the hard knocks and tired moments. But keep your eyes on the prize, and it'll happen.

Now, if you're sitting there scratching your head, not sure what your purpose is, here's a few ways to start figuring it out:

First, think about what gets you in the zone. What can you do for hours and it feels like minutes? Could be anything, from cooking to running to fixing cars. These are breadcrumbs leading you to your purpose.

Take note of what gets your gears turning. Maybe you're the go-to person for advice among your friends, or you're always tweaking gadgets. These things that come naturally to you, they're signs.

Remember those big dreams you had as a kid? Wanted to be an astronaut or a singer? Why not revisit those? Maybe there's a reason you dreamt it up in the first place.

Listen when people compliment you on something you think is no big deal. If everyone says you're great at organizing stuff or making people laugh, there's something there.

Visualize your dream life. If you picture your perfect day, what are you doing? Use that as a compass.

Talk to the people who know you best. Sometimes they see things in us we don't see in ourselves.

Got a bead on what your purpose might be? Good. Now, make it part of your routine. Set goals, break them down into steps. And keep track of your progress.

Get involved in groups with the same interests – online

communities, local clubs, workshops. Swap ideas, get inspired.

Absorb content from the folks who've already made it in the field you're interested in. Let their journey light up your path.

Say no to stuff that's not serving your purpose. Cut out the fluff.

Regularly check your goals. Make sure what you're doing every day is helping you move forward. And if it's not, don't be afraid to change things up.

It's all about staying on target, even when it feels like you're not moving. You might need to sacrifice some things, but when you look back, it'll all be worth it.

But hey, even on a purpose-driven road, you'll hit some potholes. You might lose steam or wonder if you're on the right track. That's normal. Remember, it's a journey with twists and turns.

When the going gets tough, what works for me is to plunge back into the community, listen to inspiring stories, remind myself why I started. A short break or a change of scenery can do wonders too. Gives you a fresh perspective.

Shake up your routine if things get stale. I started a podcast to talk to all sorts of successful folks, and it's been a game-changer. Keeps the ideas flowing.

Documenting your wins, the progress you've made, can give you a real boost. Seeing how far you've come is a surefire way to keep the momentum.

This path you're on, it's going to test your grit. You'll question yourself, that's guaranteed. But keep your chin up through the rough patches. Remember your 'why.' And look after yourself; burnout is a buzzkill.

Stick with it. Tend to your purpose like a garden, and watch it grow. It'll keep blooming, surprising you with rewards you didn't even know were possible. Keep watering it, and one day, you'll be living in the midst of a lush, vibrant landscape of your own making. Keep at it!

PURPOSE DISCOVERY WORKSHEET

Here's a simple worksheet that you can use to help identify and focus on your purpose.

Instructions: Feel free to write below or use a separate sheet of paper to answer the questions. Work through it at your own pace. Remember, the journey to your purpose is unique to you – there's no rush or right way to complete this worksheet.

PART 1: SELF- REFLECTION

Identify Your Passions:
List 5 activities that make you lose track of time:

1.
2.
3.
4.
5.

Childhood Dreams:
What did you dream of becoming as a child?

Skills and Compliments:
List 3 things you do well that others have complimented you on:

1.
2.
3.

Visualize Your Ideal Day:
Describe your perfect day from morning to night:

Feedback Gathering:
Ask 3 friends or family members what they think you're great at and record their responses:

1.
2.
3.

PART 2: GOAL SETTING AND PLANNING

Defining Your Purpose:
Based on your reflections, write a statement of your purpose:

Short-Term Goals:
Set 3 goals you can achieve in the next month related to your purpose:

1.
2.
3.

Long-Term Goals:
Set 3 goals you want to achieve in the next year:

1.
2.
3.

Action Steps:
For each goal, list the steps needed to achieve it:

Goal 1:
Goal 2:
Goal 3:

PART 3: COMMUNITY AND LEARNING

Community Engagement:
Identify 2-3 groups or places where like-minded individuals gather:

1.
2.

Learning Resources:
List 5 books, podcasts, or courses that can enhance your understanding of your purpose:

1.
2.
3.
4.
5.

PART 4: TRACKING AND ADJUSTMENT

Progress Tracking:
Create a weekly log to track progress towards your goals:

Regular Review:
Set a day and time each week to review your progress:

Day:

Time:

Adjustment Plan:
If progress stalls, what are two actions you can take to realign with your purpose?

1.
2.

PART 5: RESILIENCE AND SELF-CARE

Mindfulness and Self-Care:
List 3 self-care activities that help you recharge:

1.
2.
3.

Motivation Renewal:
Identify 3 things you can do when your motivation drops:

1.
2.
3.

Reflection on Challenges:
Reflect on a recent set back and write down how it made you stronger:

CHAPTER 4

Find A Mentor

Embarking on life's journey solo is a common route for many men, driven by a blend of pride and the notion of rugged individualism. But if there's a powerful connection to be made, it's the bond with a mentor. A mentor isn't just any acquaintance; they're a beacon of wisdom, having navigated the very seas we find ourselves in the midst of. I've been lucky to call several seasoned gentlemen my mentors—individuals in their golden years who've weathered the storms of life, nurturing families, cementing careers, and accumulating a trove of experiences.

Age isn't always the measure of a mentor; what counts is their having charted the territory that lies unexplored before you. With their unique vantage point, they can offer not just advice, but a compass to steer your major life decisions, providing insider insights into the trials you face. This guidance is particularly invaluable for us men who, too often, internalize our battles. A mentor then becomes the confidant, the wise counselor offering a safe harbor for the storms within, whether they pertain to relationships, career moves, or the throes of loss.

My mentors are anchors, keeping me grounded and true to my core, especially when doubt clouds my horizon. Their seasoned perspective lights up the path when all I can see is fog. The key is regular contact, not out of obligation but out of mutual respect and understanding. This isn't about transactional interactions; it's about fostering a connection that transcends the superficial, that thrives on showing up for each other in a world where such bonds are sadly rare.

When seeking a mentor, look for someone who embodies relatability, integrity, sound judgment, and patience. Communication need not be daily, but it should be intentional, particularly during those critical crossroads. Proactive engagement is better than reaching out in desperation; it's a sign of foresight and respect for the mentor's wisdom. A mentor's role isn't to hold your hand at every step but to empower you to make decisions that align with your values and aspirations.

Remember, a mentor's input is a treasure trove of lived experience —not just suggestions but life lessons hard-earned. The quest for a mentor should involve scouting for those who not only speak but demonstrate their truths through their actions. They're the ones who listen wholeheartedly, challenge you with thoughtful questions, and support you without reservation. They're your cheerleader, your sounding board, and, at times, the necessary nudge out of your comfort zone.

You might find such individuals in various settings—your workplace, a place of worship, volunteer groups, or even within your hobbies and interests. Be open to the idea that mentors can come from any walk of life and that each one can offer a distinct perspective beneficial for different facets of your growth.

In fostering a mentorship relationship, there's an art to balancing expectations. Make your goals and needs known, set a rhythm to your interactions, and ensure there's a give and take. This isn't a one-sided affair; your mentor should benefit from your growth, just as you benefit from their guidance.

And as the mentorship takes shape, bear in mind that it's about more than just solving immediate problems. It's a sustained effort to grow, to develop, and to become the man you aspire to be. Honor their time, be prepared and specific in your discussions, and take their advice to heart. Embrace the feedback, even when it challenges you, and view this relationship as complementary to your own efforts, not a replacement for your self- reliance.

If the dynamic ever shifts, communicate openly to realign your expectations. Always express gratitude and keep them updated on the positive impact they've had on your life. And when the time comes, be ready to extend what you've learned to someone else— mentoring is, after all, a cycle of passing on wisdom and fostering growth.

To summarize, a mentor is a cornerstone in the architecture of personal development, offering a unique and personalized roadmap for navigating the complexities of life. Choose wisely, engage earnestly, and in time, be ready to contribute to the cycle of growth by becoming a mentor yourself. This reciprocal exchange of wisdom isn't just a personal boon—it's a way to perpetuate a legacy of knowledge, kindness, and communal strength.

So, seek out mentors who resonate with your values, and let their experience amplify your journey. With the right people in your corner, you're not just traversing a path but paving the way for a more profound journey—not only for yourself but for those who may one day call you their mentor.

MENTOR CHECKLIST

Use this checklist to help identify a mentor to ensure you are getting the most out of your mentorship experience and that you are prepared to maintain a productive and mutually beneficial relationship with your mentor.

Identifying a Potential Mentor:
- Does the potential mentor have experience in areas you want to grow in?
- Does the individual exhibit integrity and practice what they preach?
- Is the potential mentor a good listener, providing full attention during conversations?
- Can the individual ask insightful questions that encourage you to think deeply?
- Does the mentor have a calm and grounded presence that you find encouraging?
- Is the person willing to share both their successes and failures?
- Can the mentor offer reassurance and encouragement without sugarcoating the truth?
- Is there mutual respect and potential for a two-way exchange of value?
- Does the potential mentor respect privacy and show discretion?

Once you've found a mentor, you want to make sure that you're doing what's needed to take in the lessons and get the most out of the experience. Here's a list to help:

- Do you come prepared for meetings with specific points and questions?
- Do you actively listen and take notes during discussions?
- Are you following through on agreed actions and advice from your mentor?
- Do you seek and are open to feedback, even when it is difficult to hear?
- Do you respect the mentor's time, showing up punctually for meetings and not exceeding agreed-upon time?
- Are you making an effort to apply the lessons and advice given by your mentor?
- Do you regularly express appreciation for your mentor's time and guidance?

CHAPTER 5
Transform Your Eating Habits

Transforming your diet isn't just about cutting out the bad stuff; it's a lifestyle overhaul that boosts your physical and mental vitality. If your schedule's slammed and the drive-thru's calling your name, remember: quick eats often lead to slow energy crashes.

Let's face it, I've been there. Back in my coaching days, fast food was my go-to. It seemed convenient, until my get-up-and-go got up and left. The greasy meals turned my energy to sludge and my mood to mud. The wake-up call? Realizing my diet was the culprit.

Let's get real for a second. I know the drill all too well. There I was, coaching, living that high-energy lifestyle, but my fuel choice? Fast food. Convenient, sure; it was quick, easy, and it was right there. Morning, noon, and night, I was hitting up those drive-thrus, thinking I was saving time. But here's the kicker: as my diet tanked, so did my vigor. Those meals, heavy with grease and lacking any real nutrients, started to weigh me down. It wasn't just a physical sluggishness I felt; it cast a shadow over my mood, too. It was as if my typical go-getter spirit had been buried under a pile of empty calorie wrappers.

Then one day, it hit me—like a half-eaten burger to the face. My diet wasn't just a bad habit; it was an anchor dragging me down. I had to make a change, not tomorrow, not after the next game, but right then and there.

So, I took a hard left turn from the path of least resistance. I started investing in my meals like I invested in my team's strategy. Out went the fast-food wrappers and in came the grocery bags filled with whole, unprocessed goodness. I began to fill my kitchen with a spectrum of fruits and veggies, splashes of green, bursts of berry reds, and the earthy tones of whole grains and lean proteins. These weren't just ingredients; they were the building blocks of a new lifestyle.

This wasn't an overnight flip. It took trial and error, figuring out that kale could actually taste good and that quinoa wasn't just a fancy rice. I learned how to season and savor the natural goodness of food, how to appreciate the crunch of a fresh apple over the crunch of a deep-fried fry. Slowly but surely, the weight of my old diet lifted, and my energy levels started to climb. I could feel a difference in my morning jog, my focus during game plays, and my patience with my team.

But this transformation was more than just a physical one. Mentally, I felt clearer, like I'd cleaned the windshield to my brain. Emotionally, I found myself more balanced, more even-tempered. It turned out that what I ate didn't just fuel my body; it fueled my entire being.

I started to understand that eating well could be the norm, not the exception. It became less about what I was giving up and more about what I was gaining. And as I made these shifts, the proof was there, staring back at me in the mirror, ticking away in my watch's lap times, and in the nods of respect from my team who saw their coach walking the talk.

Switching gears, I swapped out the fried and fake for fresh and nutritious. Fruits, veggies, lean meats, and whole grains didn't just change my plate; they changed my performance—both in my head and in my heart.

Here's the real talk: indulgences are fine, but don't let them be your dietary staple. Men, it's time we took our nutrition as seriously as our workouts. Your diet is the fuel for life's marathon, not just a sprint to the next meal.

So, take a hard look at your plate. Is it more processed than fresh? Is water an afterthought? Are veggies strangers to your meals? Start by ditching the worst offenders—those sugary drinks, the daily red meat, and anything with a sugar content that's through the roof.

Meal prepping on weekends isn't just for fitness buffs; it's for any guy who wants to avoid the temptation of the takeout line. Trust me, your Monday self will thank you.

And when you do eat, think color—nature's palette is a cheat sheet for nutrient-rich foods. Stuff like dark, leafy greens, bright berries, and the rainbow array of vegetables should be regulars on your plate. They're not just good for you; they make meals more enjoyable.

Carbs are friends, not foes, but pick the ones that stick with you, like oats, brown rice, and legumes. And fats? They're essential, but go for the heart- healthy kinds like nuts, avocados, and olive oil.

Hydration is key, but let's be honest, water can be boring. Keep it interesting with slices of lemon, lime, or cucumber, and swap out the sugary sodas for herbal teas or sparkling water.

When you're browsing the grocery store aisles, the ingredient lists on food packages can be filled with unpronounceable terms. Often, they read more like a science experiment than a recipe for something edible. If the list is littered with mysterious additives, artificial flavors, and preservatives, it's usually a sign to steer clear. The principle here is straightforward: if it sounds like it belongs in a science experiment rather than in your body, it's wise to leave it on the shelf. Opt instead for foods with simple, recognizable ingredients – things your grandmother would have had in her kitchen.

Now, you might think that making your own food staples is a task reserved for those with too much time on their hands, but it's not as intimidating as it appears. With a little planning and some basic techniques, you can whip up homemade bread, granola, nut butters, and even condiments like ketchup or mustard. Not only will you have complete control over what goes into your food – no hidden sugars, salts, or preservatives – but you'll also notice a significant bump in the quality and flavor of your meals.
It's empowering to know exactly what you're eating and satisfying to enjoy something you've made from scratch.

The benefits go beyond the nutritional aspect. There's a particular joy in the act of creating something with your own hands – it connects you to your food in a way that buying pre-packaged items never can. Plus, there's the economic advantage: often, making your own staples can be more cost- effective in the long run.

Yes, it takes time to knead dough, monitor the rise of your bread, or stir a pot of simmering fruit for jam, but the process can be therapeutic, almost meditative. In our high-speed world, slowing down to craft something as fundamental as the food we eat is a quiet act of rebellion against the convenience-over-quality culture. And let's not forget the bragging rights that come with pulling a freshly baked loaf of bread out of the oven. The enticing aroma alone is worth the effort, and when you slice into it, you'll know it's made of ingredients that serve your body well.

Begin with something small – maybe a simple loaf of bread or a batch of granola – and as you get comfortable, your culinary repertoire will naturally expand. Each homemade staple is a step towards a healthier lifestyle, one that prizes substance over convenience, wholesomeness over haste.

Remember, transforming your diet isn't a sprint; it's a marathon with pit stops and hurdles along the way.

Here's the game plan:

- Aim for progress, not perfection. One better choice at a time adds up.
- Notice how good nutrition changes the game for your body and mind.
- Get your crew involved—eating right's easier when you're not going solo.
- Prep like a pro on weekends; it'll save you from midweek mayhem.
- Keep healthy snacks on hand to dodge those hunger-driven mistakes.
- Treat yourself, but keep it to a treat, not a regular beat.
- Track the wins, like that extra mile you ran or adding a vegetable with your meal.
- Ditch the "good" vs. "bad" food guilt trip—balance is your buddy.
- If you slip, no sweat. The next meal's your comeback.

It's about feeling pumped, slashing those health risks, and, let's be honest, setting a prime example for the folks looking up to you.

Kickstart this journey today. Because the best project you'll ever work on is you.

CHAPTER 6
Prioritize Your Health

It's no secret that many of us guys are a bit stubborn about seeing the doctor. We're pros at playing down the aches and ignoring the signals our bodies send us. Yet, embracing regular checkups and screenings is essential – it's not just about catching things early; it's about staying ahead of the game when it comes to our health. Brushing off symptoms or fearing what might be found only does us a disservice.

Sure, nobody wants to hear they've got a health issue. It's tempting to live in blissful ignorance, but here's the real deal: the earlier a problem is caught, the easier it usually is to manage or fix. Waiting until you're feeling lousy? Not the best strategy. Regular doctor visits give you the lowdown on your health, and there's genuine peace of mind when the news is good.

Some guys have this idea that docs will wave off their concerns, or that visits aren't needed if you're feeling shipshape. But regular checkups are not just about how you're feeling today – they're about ensuring you stay feeling good tomorrow, too. They're a chance to establish a health baseline and to catch potential issues that aren't on your radar yet.

I get it, though. In some communities, there's a real history of mistrust towards healthcare, and not without reason. But believe me, there are doctors out there who get it – who listen, respect, and genuinely want to see you at your healthiest. Finding a good one can be a game-changer.

Take it from me: I'm pretty tight with my doc. She's been my go-to for years, always taking the time to talk things through and making sure I understand what's up with my health. We've built a solid doc-patient relationship that didn't happen overnight, but man, it's been worth it.

I'm in for a physical once a year and get labs done periodically. Keeping tabs on things like cholesterol and blood sugar is my way of staying in the driver's seat when it comes to my health. It's all about laying the groundwork to stay spry and healthy for the long haul.

So let's ditch the outdated notion that toughing it out is the manly way. Being proactive about your health is smart. It means you're playing the long game – staying fit for yourself and those who count on you.

In the gap between acknowledging the importance of proactive health management and diving into the practical ways to maintain physical health, there is a crucial component that often goes overlooked, especially among men: mental health. Just as our bodies require regular checkups and maintenance, our minds need the same level of care and attention to stay well.

For too long, society has peddled the narrative that men must always be strong and unaffected, that emotional resilience means silencing our struggles, and that vulnerability is a sign of weakness. This kind of thinking is not just outdated, it's harmful. It's a barrier to seeking help and can feed mental health problems. It's time to change the conversation and recognize that mental toughness also includes taking care of our psychological well being.

Mental health is an integral part of the long game for overall wellness. It's about ensuring you're not just physically fit, but also mentally robust to face life's challenges. Mental fitness means having the emotional and cognitive resources to navigate stress, make decisions, and connect with others in meaningful ways.

Here's the thing: mental health issues don't discriminate. They can affect anyone, regardless of strength, age, or race. But what we can control is how we respond. Do we bottle up our feelings and risk compounding the stress? Or do we reach out, speak up, and seek support when needed? This is where true strength lies.

Men, it's okay not to be okay. It's okay to say you're struggling and to ask for help. This could mean talking to a trusted friend or family member, seeking support from a mental health professional, or even exploring online resources and support networks. There are many forms of therapy, from traditional one-on-one sessions to group therapy, and even online platforms that offer counseling and support.

Remember, your mental health is just as important as your physical health. It affects how you think, feel, and behave daily. It impacts your ability to handle stress, relate to others, and make choices. By taking care of your mental health, you're ensuring that you're there for yourself and your loved ones not just physically, but emotionally and mentally as well.

So before we move on to the checklist for physical health, let's add a mental health check-in there. How are you feeling? What's weighing on your mind? Have you given yourself permission to prioritize your emotional wellbeing? Addressing these questions can help you stay balanced and focused, enabling you to engage in the practical aspects of health with a clear and prepared mind. Now, for the practical stuff.

Here's my checklist for staying on top of your health game:

1. Hunt down a good primary care doc – check reviews and find someone who fits.
2. Book that annual physical early – make it non-negotiable in your calendar.
3. Keep a running list of any weird or new symptoms and talk them through with your doc.

4. Demand clear explanations – no jargon, please. And if something's prescribed, know what it is and why you're taking it.
5. Your family's health history? It matters. Have it down pat for yourself and your kids.
6. Lifestyle checks – are you moving enough, sleeping well, managing stress, eating right? Your doc should be in that loop.
7. If something comes up, go full detective mode – research, ask questions, and yes, a second opinion never hurts.
8. Specialists aren't just for severe cases – sometimes they're the best preventative step.
9. Hit up support groups or therapists if health issues start to weigh heavy.
10. Build a supportive community and practice openness about health challenges to foster resilience and well-being.

Listen, I know life's hectic and doctor's appointments can feel like one more thing on an endless to-do list. But try to look at this as non-negotiable, like changing the oil in your car to keep it running smoothly. And hey, if money's tight, talk to your doctor's office. There's often wiggle room or payment plans, and telehealth or after-hours appointments can fit even the craziest schedule.

Feeling nervous? That's normal. Open up about it to your doctor – it's their job to ease those nerves. Bringing along a friend or a family member that can help too.

Think of health maintenance as an investment, with dividends paid in quality of life. It's not about being perfect; it's about consistent care. If you falter, no sweat – just pick up where you left off. Your health is your wealth, fellas. Take charge of it, and your future self will be grateful.

CHAPTER 7

Make Time For Physical Activity

Exercise is one of the most important habits for maintaining health as we age. But with increasingly sedentary lifestyles, many men struggle to stay active. In this chapter, I'll share practical tips to build more movement into your day.

I've made fitness a priority for decades, but it's still easy to slip into stretches of inactivity when life gets busy. Work pressures ramp up. Family obligations pile on. By the end of the day, exhaustion sets in. Motivation to work out fades.

But I've learned that even small amounts of exercise make a big difference. On days when I can't seem to fit in a full workout, I'll take mini-breaks throughout my workday to stretch or do some squats. Or I'll squeeze in a 30-minute home yoga video before bed.

Staying active helps me manage stress better, sleep more soundly, and maintain a healthy weight. Exercise also reduces my back pain and knee soreness that can come with aging. I feel more confident and energetic when I move consistently.

Start by taking an honest look at your current activity level. Are you sitting for prolonged periods? Do you rely heavily on cars instead of walking? How often do you intentionally get your heart rate up?

Then set realistic goals for adding more movement into your days.

Even starting with 20-30 minutes of moderate exercise can make a difference. Go for a walk, follow workout videos online, dance around your living room - anything to get moving!

Consistency matters more than intensity. The key is establishing exercise as a daily habit, whatever form it takes. Your health is worth carving out the time.

Finding ways to exercise more consistently requires some creativity and commitment. Personally, I've found it helpful to schedule workouts on my calendar so they don't get pushed aside by other priorities. Setting reminders on my phone also keeps me accountable to stick with my routine.

It's important to find forms of exercise you genuinely enjoy. That way it feels less like an obligation or chore. I've grown to love swimming laps and riding bikes outdoors. But something like Zumba classes energizes some of my friends. Figure out what moves you, literally and figuratively!

Having workout buddies or accountability partners can make fitness more engaging too. My neighbor and I meet up twice a week for strength training in his home gym. And a couple of coworkers join me for evening walks when the weather is nice. Support from others helps consistency.

I also discovered that switching up my activities kept me from getting bored. I'll lift weights one day, go for a run the next, and maybe try a dance aerobics video after that. Variety prevents exercise ruts.

On days when my schedule is jammed, I've learned to take advantage of little pockets of time for mini-workouts. Just 10 minutes of squats and pushups between conference calls adds up. Look for natural movement opportunities like parking farther away or taking the stairs.

When I'm working out solo, listening to energetic music, podcasts or audiobooks makes the time pass quickly. Find ways to make exercise as entertaining as possible!

Above all, focus on consistency rather than quantity. Perfecting your form with squats or plank holds for a few minutes daily provides benefits over the long-term. You don't have to overdo it initially. Slow and steady!

Recognize the barriers to exercise, like work and family commitments, and find ways to overcome them. Acknowledge that small bouts of activity are beneficial and set achievable goals for physical movement. Here are some quick tips:

- **Assess and Adjust**: Take stock of how much you move each day and look for opportunities to increase activity
- **Start Small**: Begin with short, manageable workouts that fit into your schedule, aiming for consistency over intensity.
- **Calendar Commitment**: Block out time for exercise in your calendar as you would any important appointment.
- **Find Joy in Movement**: Choose activities you enjoy to ensure you look forward to your workout sessions.
- **Buddy Up**: Exercise with a friend or join a group to stay motivated.
- **Mix It Up**: Keep your routine interesting by varying your activities.
- **Seize Every Moment**: Use short breaks throughout the day for quick exercises like squats or stretches.
- **Entertain as You Train**: Listen to music or podcasts to make solo workouts fly by.
- **Small Efforts Count**: Even minimal movement adds up, so don't discount the little things.
- **Stay Mindful**: Pay attention to your body's signals and be willing to adjust your routines to avoid injury.

Commit to exercise for your health first and foremost - aesthetics will follow. Devote time to self-care through daily movement. Remind yourself that you deserve to feel strong and energetic.

Tune in to how working out improves your physical and mental wellbeing. Let those be your motivators. Gradually increase your baseline for what types of fitness challenges feel doable. You've got this!

Here are some convenient and simple workout ideas for every day men with different lifestyles:

Desk Job Guy - office worker, remote worker, programmers, call center, etc.

- Set a reminder to take a 5 minute walking break every hour - walk around office or outside
- Do seated leg raises and calf raises while on phone calls
- Keep resistance bands at your desk for arm curls and shoulder presses during breaks
- Stand up to stretch your hips,hamstrings and back periodically
- Do push ups against the wall during phone calls - aim for 10-15 reps
- During lunch, take 10-15 minutes to walk outside or do some bodyweight squats
- Stay hydrated and fuel up with healthy snacks to power through busy days

Driver Guy - delivery driver, truck driver, bus drivers, taxi/rideshare drivers, salesman

- Park farther away from entrances to get extra walking steps in
- While stopped at a light or in traffic, do shoulder shrugs and neck stretches
- Keep a resistance band in your vehicle to do arm exercises like bicep curls at red lights
- Take mini walking breaks every couple of hours to restore circulation
- Do seated calf raises during breaks
- Replace sitting with standing/light movement during phone calls when possible
- Stay hydrated and fuel up with healthy snacks to power through busy days

On-the-Go Guy - construction, medical, landscapers, teachers, etc.

- Take the stairs whenever you can throughout the day
- Walk or bike to nearby places instead of driving
- Map out walking routes for meetings instead of taxis/transit
- Do quick routines like 3 sets of 5 squats, lunges or push-ups whenever free time opens up for you.
- Stay hydrated and fuel up with healthy snacks to power through busy days
- The key is finding little ways to move more that work with your specific lifestyle. Consistency pays off over time.

CHAPTER 8

Trust Your Gut & Surround Yourself With Positivity

As men, we often override our inner guidance and do what we "should" do instead. We dismiss intuition in favor of social conditioning or mental resistance. But listening to your inner voice is crucial for well-being.

I spent years distracting myself from my own wisdom. I filled my schedule with busyness to avoid reflecting. I wrote off unease around certain people as being overly skeptical. I reasoned that I could muscle through anything solo.

The truth? That way of living was exhausting and unsustainable. I felt constantly on edge, like I had to prove my strength. My mind was cluttered with everyone else's expectations. I lost touch with my own needs.

It took me too long to realize I needed to tune out the noise and listen within. Your inner voice always guides you towards what's right for YOU, not what your parents, friends or society dictated. It knows your truth.

Start paying attention to your intuition - that gut sense about a decision or about someone's intentions. Don't override it just because the practical mind downplays it. Lean into your inner wisdom.

This goes for all areas of life. Is your job draining your soul? Is a relationship unhealthy? Does anxiety build about a choice? Check those reactions. Your inner voice knows.

Making space for self-reflection allows your truth to surface. Meditation, journaling, long walks in nature are all pathways. Unplug regularly from devices and external stimulation.

Begin valuing your own counsel over everyone else's. Your intuition is a gift, your compass for living a life that honors your spirit. Keep tuning in.

Tuning into your inner voice and trusting your intuition is a process that takes dedication, patience and compassion towards yourself. At first, it can be challenging to separate your core wisdom from the practical mind's resistance or society's expectations. Self-doubt also often arises as we try to connect to our truth.

I recommend starting small by scheduling brief pockets of time for reflection each day or week. Even 5-10 minutes of meditation, journaling or being in nature can help calm your mind. The more you create space to tune out distractions and listen within, the easier it becomes.
Don't judge the messages that surface, but rather observe them with openness and curiosity. Your inner voice is your ally, not your adversary. Making note of the guidance you receive helps integrate those insights into your consciousness.

It's important not to override intuition just because it contradicts pragmatic thinking. Your inner wisdom stems from a deeper place of innate knowing. When facing big decisions, check that choices align with your core values before moving forward.

This process is greatly strengthened by the community. Discussing insights with supportive friends allows you to gain perspective. We all have blind spots that others can help illuminate. Mutual sharing builds trust in your own inner voice.

With consistent practice, your connection to your inner truth will grow stronger. Learn to recognize and release any self-doubt or shame that arises. Be patient and appreciative - this is a gift that supports your journey. Keep listening within.

As you strengthen your connection to your inner voice, keep these final tips in mind:

- Be patient and compassionate with yourself - this skill takes practice.
- Don't override intuition just because it contradicts practical thinking.
- Check in frequently - once a day or week to start. Make it a habit.
- Write down the guidance you receive to integrate the insights.
- Don't judge the messages - just observe them with curiosity.
- Confirm decisions align with your values before moving forward.
- Catch self-doubt arising and reframe it - "I know and trust myself."
- If you feel guilt or shame surface, release it - you are enough.
- Discuss insights with supportive friends-get their perspective.
- Appreciate your inner voice as your greatest guide - it has your back.

Learning to listen within requires dedication in the face of distractions. But the clarity and confidence you'll cultivate by following your inner wisdom is invaluable.

Quiet the mind chatter and tap into your core. Let your truth guide your actions, relationships and direction. The possibilities will unfold powerfully.

Here are some tips for strengthening your connection to your inner voice:

- **Make listening to your intuition a consistent daily practice.** Even taking just 5 minutes in the morning to check in with yourself and set intentions can make a difference over time. Practicing tuning into your inner guidance throughout the day, even in small moments, will help it become second nature. When you start second-guessing a decision, pause and get grounded by taking some deep breaths. Imagine your feet on the floor and calmly ask yourself - what does my heart say? Don't let anxiety overwhelm your inner wisdom.

- **Pay close attention to how your body responds to various situations and people.** Tension, fatigue or discomfort can actually be your intuition's way of signaling its alerts. On the flip side, relaxation, joy and openness in your body can affirm you're on the right path. Trust actions over empty words, both your own behavior and that of others. Make sure what you do aligns with your truth, not just what you say. And look at people's deeds rather than just their promises. Your gut knows when something feels off.

- **Surround yourself with encouraging friends who empower you to honor your authentic self.** Their support helps drown out the negative and critical inner voices we all battle at times. Be cautious of relationships that pressure you to ignore your needs and wisdom. Reflect on past experiences where you didn't listen to your intuition - what lessons can you draw about how following your inner voice may have led to better outcomes?

- **Meet yourself with kindness as you get back right,** when you've messed up or gone off track. Guilt and shame will only muffle your inner wisdom further. Everything is a learning experience - keep nurturing your connection with patience. Make listening to your heart a non-negotiable daily priority. Respect your inner voice as the compass guiding you towards your best life. Keep tuning in!

AFTERWORD

As I wrap this up, I can't help but feel truly blessed. This week, my son is starting college—a momentous occasion that fills me with pride and honor. I've always admired his resilience, his toughness, his strong character. He's a Christian, a leader, and he's got this disciplined approach to working out that really sets him apart.

But it's not just about him. I'm surrounded by incredible people, a network of friends who are nothing short of amazing. These are the kind of guys who would give you their last, genuine and quality individuals. And speaking of mentorship, I'm grateful to have found mentors for my son as he was growing up. I wanted to ensure that, despite how cool I thought I was, he had solid role models from different generations guiding him. These are strong men with shared values who care deeply for him, men who aren't obsessed with material wealth.

And you know what's really refreshing? My friendships with younger guys. They keep me connected to the current scene. I've never been the type to resent those coming up behind me. I appreciate young players because they'll eventually become the experienced ones, guiding the next generation. It's a cycle that keeps things fresh and exciting.

Now, a quick note about language. Let's try to keep the cursing to a minimum. I know, it's a bit of an old habit, but cutting back on the strong language can help spread positivity and make our message more accessible to everyone.

I genuinely appreciate all of you. May God bless each one of you. Take care.

ABOUT THE AUTHOR

Coach John Louden

Coach John Louden, born in Gary, Indiana, was raised in a community that nurtured his early aspirations. However, his youthful indiscretions led him to learn difficult life lessons, culminating in a loss of freedom during his formative years. This period of incarceration became a turning point for Coach Louden. He crafted a plan to redeem himself and honor the memory of his late mother, who had sadly passed away without witnessing her son's transformation.

Today, Coach Louden is a beacon of positive change, sharing his journey from a tumultuous past to a fulfilling present. He has evolved from a life of uncertainty to one brimming with purpose and success. As a family man, businessman, entrepreneur, coach, mentor, community leader, and volunteer, Coach Louden embodies the potential for personal growth and transformation.

In his role as a coach and mentor, Coach Louden is committed to guiding others on their paths to self-improvement and success. His story is a powerful testament to the possibility of turning life's challenges into opportunities for prosperity. Coach Louden's narrative is an inspiring example of how personal change begins within and can profoundly impact one's life and community.